For Phoebe the great.
And the bears, one through eight.
—J.H.

For Nicole, and Phoebe,
and Bears . . . oh my!
—L.K.

Text copyright © 2023 by Joan Holub
Jacket art and interior illustrations copyright © 2023 by Laurie Keller

All rights reserved. Published in the United States by Crown Books for Young Readers,
an imprint of Random House Children's Books, a division of Penguin Random House LLC, New York.

Crown and the colophon are registered trademarks of Penguin Random House LLC.

Visit us on the Web! rhcbooks.com

Educators and librarians, for a variety of teaching tools, visit us at RHTeachersLibrarians.com

Library of Congress Cataloging-in-Publication Data is available upon request.
ISBN 978-0-525-64533-7 (hardcover)—ISBN 978-0-525-64534-4 (lib. bdg.)
ISBN 978-0-525-64535-1 (ebook)

The text of this book is set in Sugary Pancake.
The illustrations in this book were created using traditional and digital collage.
Book design by Nicole de las Heras

MANUFACTURED IN CHINA   10 9 8 7 6 5 4 3 2 1   First Edition

Random House Children's Books supports
the First Amendment and celebrates the right to read.

BEARS ARE BEST!

written by
Joan Holub

illustrated by
Laurie Keller

Crown Books for Young Readers ♛ New York

GRRREETINGS!

My name is Brown Bear.

I AM THE ONLY BEAR IN THIS BOOK!

Yes, I am.

I'm Brown Bear.
Behold my fur and paws.
Beware my claws!
I am the only bear in
this book . . . and that's
how I like it.
What's your name?

Name's Polar Bear.
Bear?
Mm-hmm. I have paws and claws. Fur too. It keeps me warm in the snow and ice where I live.

I live in forests, mountain meadows, and woodlands. I have a hump between my shoulders. You don't. We are different. So how can we *both* be bears?

I'm bigger than you. And I have little bumps on the bottoms of my paws to keep me from slipping on the ice. You don't. We *are* different. But we can both be bears.

You do *smell* like a bear. Too bad you do not smell like food. I could go for some honey right now.
sniff sniff
sniff sniff sniff sniff sniff sniff
Bears have one of the best senses of smell of any animal. I can smell a seal half a mile away. I wish you smelled like a seal. Because . . . yum.

Wait! I figured it out. You came to steal my food, didn't you? Well, I know how to scare you off. Watch this!
Say what? I don't even like honey.

I'LL cLack my teeth, huff, and sLap the ground.

That means I want you to go away. Although I don't defend territory like a wolf does, I do like to be by myself.

Same.

Grrr. So you still think *you* are the bear?

Duh. Does a bear poop in the woods? I *know* I'm a bear. But maybe there's room for two bears in this book?

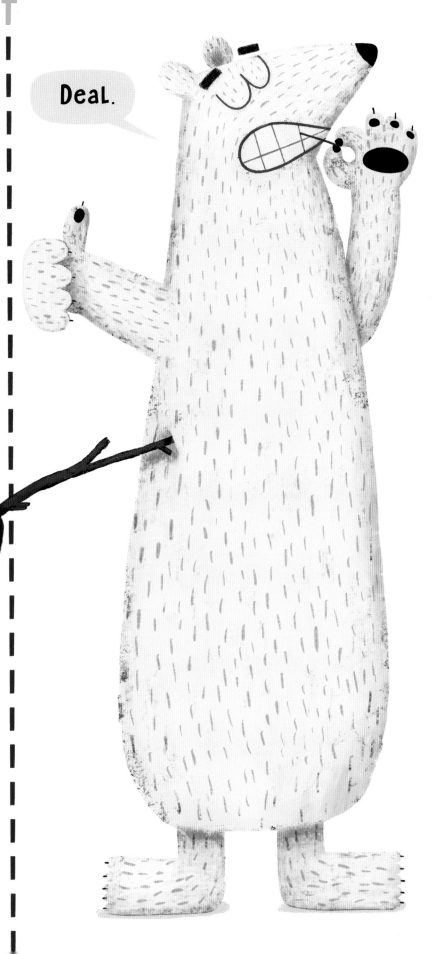

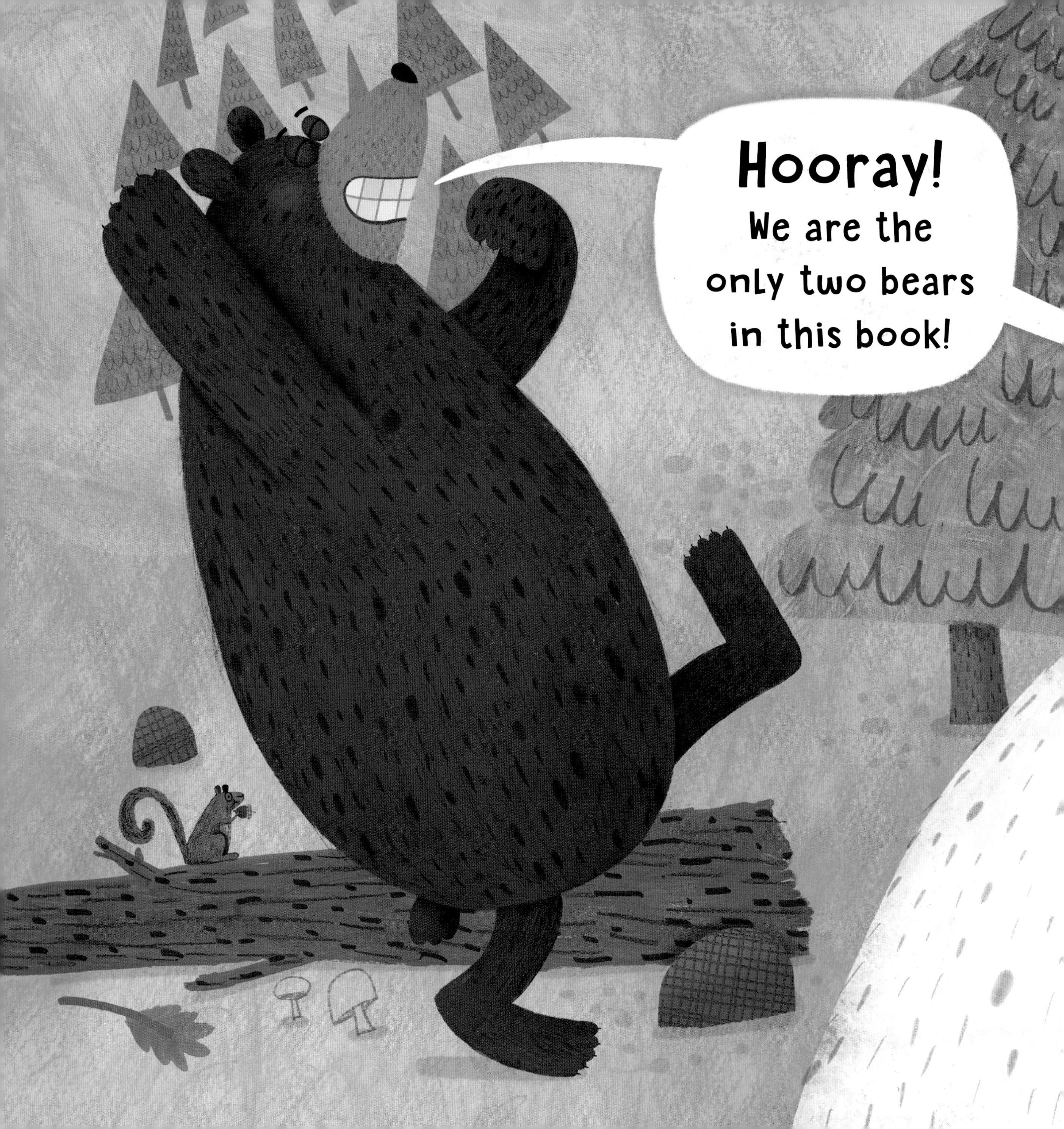
Hooray!
We are the
only two bears
in this book!

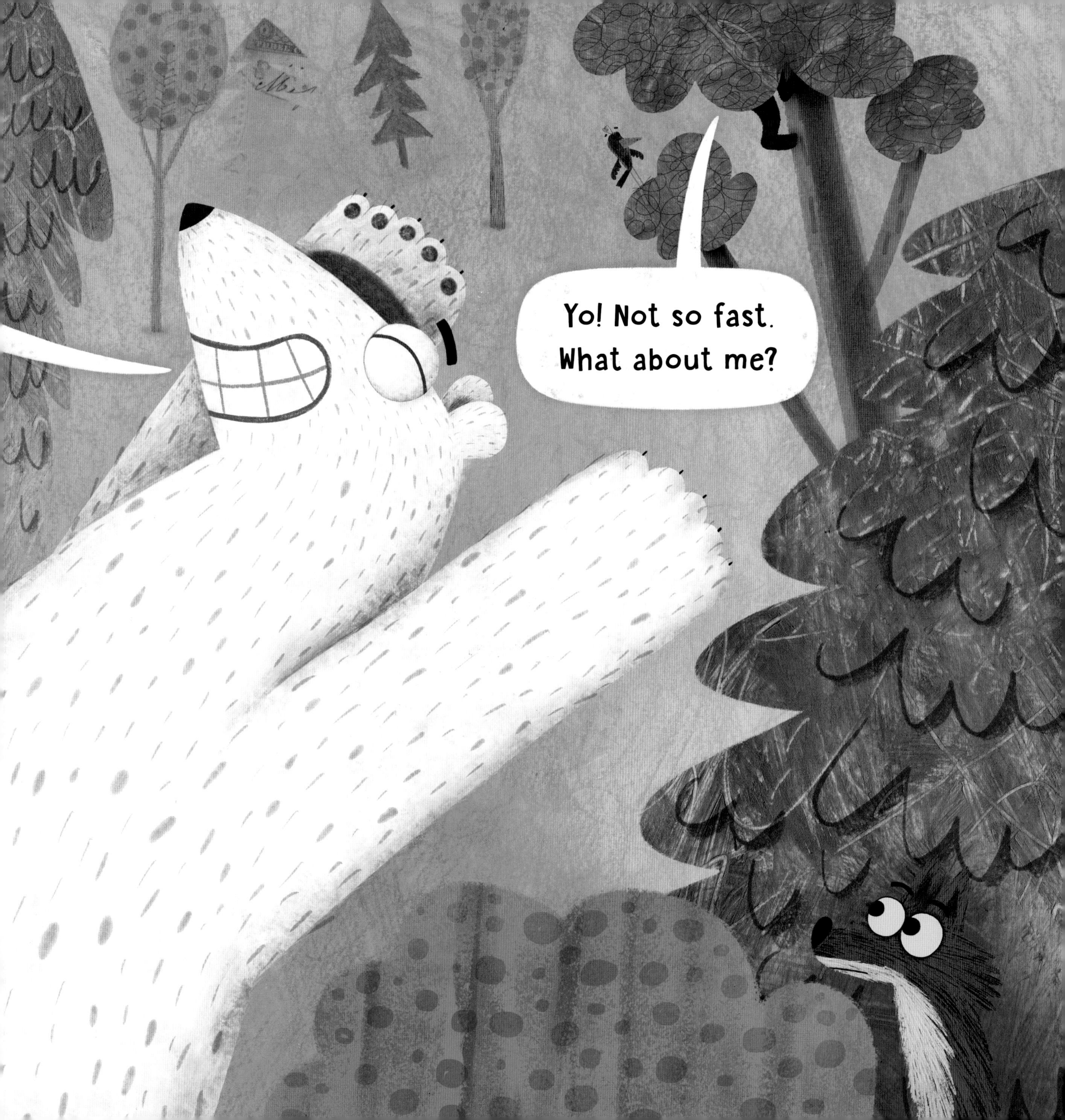
Yo! Not so fast.
What about me?

Who are you?
I'm American Black Bear. I'm a great tree-climber, thanks to my strong, short, curved claws.
I stink at climbing trees. I'm a great swimmer, though.
Three bears in one book? It's getting to be like that Goldilocks story in here.

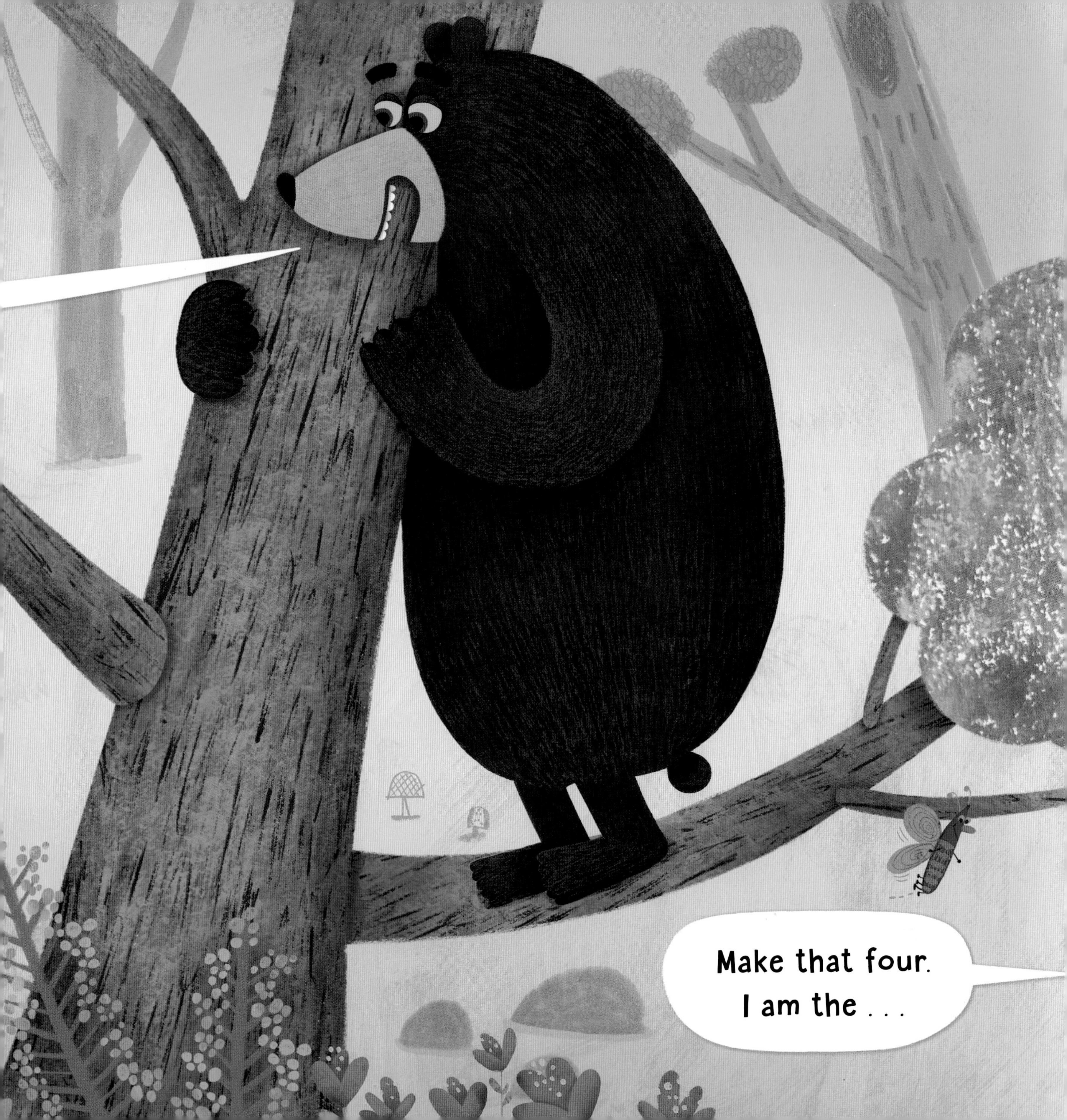
Make that four.
I am the . . .

. . . Bear?
YES.
How did you guess?
Sloth Bear's my name.
I've got cool claws, too.
They're C-shaped and good
for ripping into trees and
mounds to find insects.

There's a hole in my smile where my two front teeth are missing. See? In one meal, I can suck in 10,000 tasty termites through it! Just doing my part to keep the insect population in check. It's my bear duty.

Bear? Did someone call me?

I am the bear!
Join the club.
Club? Is that like some kind of bear party? Because I'm not really a party animal. I don't usually like to hang out with others.
None of us do.
Okay, well, since you're here . . . I'm Spectacled Bear. So called because I've got spectacular cream-colored circles around my eyes that look like big spectacles. (That's a fancy word for glasses.)

Hey, what happened to staying on your side of the page?
No room anymore.
Yoo-hoo!

Hi! I'm Sun Bear. I'm nocturnal. That means I sleep by day and search for food at night. So I don't see the actual sun all that often. I'm the smallest bear.
But I've got the longest tongue of any bear–ten inches!
I'm diurnal–active during the day unless too many people, predators, or other bears are nearby.

Dudes!
Don't forget us.
Oh no! I think I smell even more bears up ahead. So don't turn the–

I'm Giant Panda, the only bear with a thumb-like bone on each front paw. Thumbs come in handy for holding bamboo stalks. I spend twelve hours a day eating this stuff!
You're not really all that giant, though.
True. He's the second smallest bear, after me.
Wish I had thumbs.
Me too.

I'm Asiatic Black Bear. I'm the most bipedal bear, which means I can walk on two legs for longer than the rest of you.
It's getting *way* too crowded around here.

BROWN • POLAR • AMERICAN BLACK • SLOTH • SPECTACLED • SUN • GIANT PANDA • ASIATIC BLACK •

STOP!
NO MORE BEARS!
There are officially only eight species (kinds) in this book, and in the whole world. That's *all!*

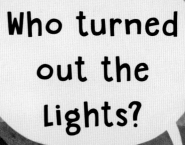

LIST?
Grrreat idea, bears!
Let's make a list of things
that are the same about us.
Otherwise, anyone could
say they are a bear.

I just thought up a
joke: What do you call
bears with no ears?
B!

EIGHT THINGS THAT MAKE A BEAR A BEAR:

1. Our shape
Big heads, small eyes (usually brown),
round ears, and short tails

2. Four paws, each with five claws
Bears walk on four legs. Sometimes we stand or walk a short way on two.
We are pigeon-toed, with our front feet turned inward.
We have claws for fighting, climbing, digging, grooming our fur,
and getting or holding food. Cats can pull their claws in, but we can't.

3. Fur
Fur protects us from bug bites and
stings and from scratchy branches.
It also keeps us warm.

4. Mammals
Like human babies, we drink milk
when we are cubs. Our moms
usually birth two or three cubs at
once. A newborn bear cub weighs
about one pound, can't see yet,
and is mostly bald.

5. Fast runners
Bears can run up to thirty-five miles per hour.
The fastest human can run
twenty-seven miles per hour.

6. Curious
We're smart and very curious.
This can get us in trouble if we wander
too close to humans. Humans should
never feed or go near a bear.

7. Good noses
Smell is our best sense. We can smell
seven times better than a bloodhound
that's able to track lost people by scent.
Our noses can find friends, enemies,
family, home, and . . .

sniff sniff

What's that smell?

. . . FOOD!
Wait, hold your seahorses! What's number eight?

8. Big eaters!

Bears spend more time finding and getting food than doing anything else. We are predators—animals that eat other animals. But bears also eat plants. (Depends on what foods we can find where we live.) That makes us omnivores.

Here are some of our favorite foods:

I Lurve iceberg-ers. Ha-ha! Just kidding. I'd like a seal for my meal.

Bamboo, bamboo, and more bamboo! It's 99 percent of what I eat.

Berries, roots, grasses, and ants rock! I also like fish, honey, and the occasional mouse.

Pass the pineapples and coconuts, please.
Fruits, berries, honey, insects, and bring on the lizards.
I'll take insects, fruit, honey, nuts, seeds, and beehives.
I'm big on termites and ants. Maybe with a side of fruits and veggies.
TERMITE TRAIL MIX
I like honey, berries, and fish! But I'm not picky and will try almost any food.

Snowflakes!

Winter's coming. Bears are especially hungry before and after hibernation—how some of us survive cold weather when it's hard to find food. While hibernating, we sleep for weeks or months without eating, drinking, peeing, or pooping. Our heartbeats and breathing slow down. We stay in a safe place and save our energy till springtime.

I think it's time for you guys to head home. (Hint, hint.)

Surprise!

Hee Hee

Whee

Thunk!

Bears live in North America, South America, Europe, and Asia.

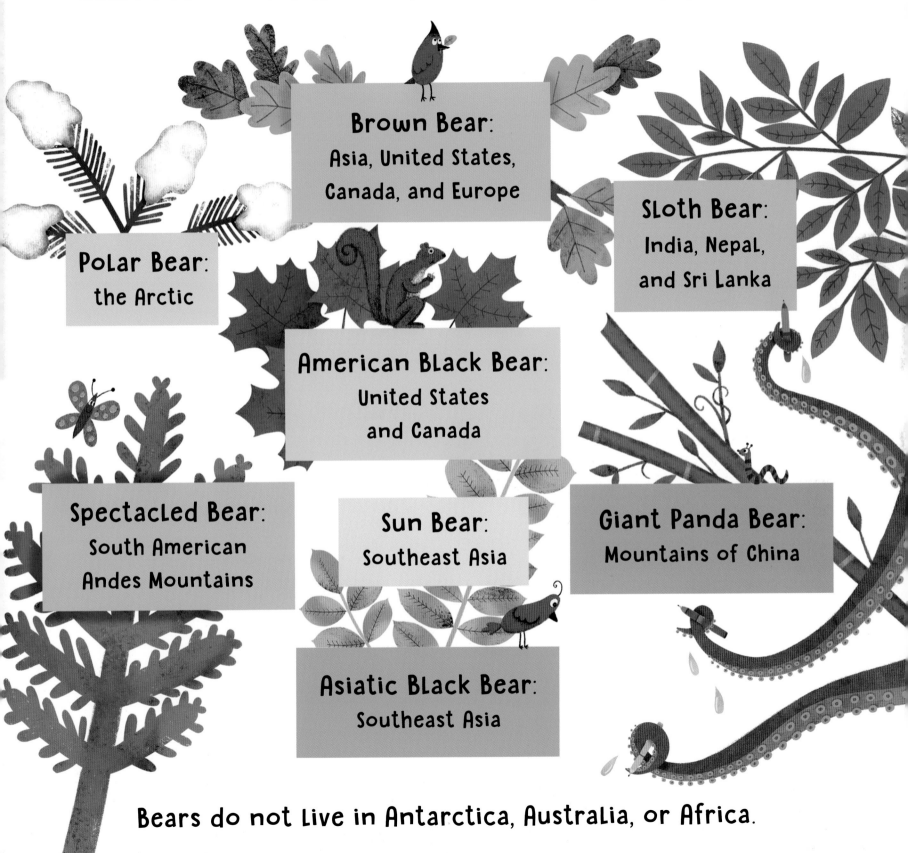

Brown Bear:
Asia, United States, Canada, and Europe

Sloth Bear:
India, Nepal, and Sri Lanka

Polar Bear:
the Arctic

American Black Bear:
United States and Canada

Spectacled Bear:
South American Andes Mountains

Sun Bear:
Southeast Asia

Giant Panda Bear:
Mountains of China

Asiatic Black Bear:
Southeast Asia

Bears do not live in Antarctica, Australia, or Africa.

Before we take off—
GROUP BEAR HUG!*
*The only time in history all eight kinds of bears have ever hugged it out.
I'm gonna hibernate. I've got a cave all picked out. How about you guys?
Yes! Hibernate!
HiberNOT!
HiberNOT! In winter, I just move down my mountain to where it's warmer.

HiberNOT! I'm used to the cold. (But polar bear moms-to-be sometimes hibernate.)
In warm areas, I don't hibernate. In cold areas, I do.
HiberNOT!
HiberNOT!

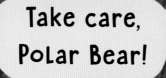

See ya around, Brown.
It's been fun, Sun! So Long!
Beary nice meeting you!
I will sort of miss those guys. They were awesome pawsome! On the bright side . . .
Adios!

Now I am the only bear
in this book again!

I'm snuggling into my cave now.
It's so nice and quiet.
Plenty of time to dream about food.
And to read, relax, or do
whatever I want.
Friends are the beary best.

But everyone needs
alone time.

And that's okay.

There are eight species of bears. Brown Bear, Polar Bear, and the American Black Bear are the most common. Many bears help the earth by eating plants. Their poop scatters the seeds to grow new plants. They also eat insects and animals, which helps balance how many and what kinds of creatures live in their habitats.

POLAR BEAR:
I look white because my fur—which is colorless—reflects light. Underneath, my skin is black. I live in the Arctic near the North Pole, which is how I got my name. I can weigh 1,500 pounds and am the biggest bear.

BROWN BEAR:
I'm the only bear with a hump of strong muscles between my shoulders. It makes me a powerful digger. Grizzly and Kodiak Bears are subspecies of Brown Bears.

SPECTACLED BEAR:
I'm also called Andean Bear because I live in the jungles of the Andes Mountains in South America. I'm one of the most arboreal bears, which means I spend a lot of time in trees. I build platforms in their branches where I eat or sleep.

AMERICAN BLACK BEAR:
There are more of me than any other kind of bear. My front paws can do things that people's hands can do, like opening jars. Subspecies called Spirit Bears or Glacier Bears have white or silver-blue fur.

SUN BEAR:

I got my name from the golden patch of fur on my chest that looks like a rising sun. I'm nicknamed Honey Bear, because I love honey, and Dog Bear, because some people think I look like a dog. At 60–150 pounds, I'm the smallest bear.

BROWN BEAR CLAW, ACTUAL SIZE

ASIATIC BLACK BEAR:

I have a collar of fur around my neck that looks like a lion's mane. Because of the creamy-white half-moon shape in my chest fur, I'm also called Moon Bear.

SLOTH BEAR:

I only have forty teeth. Other bears have forty-two. I can shut my nostrils to stop insects from getting in my nose while I gobble them. When I vacuum termites, it's so loud that I can be heard 300 feet away!

GIANT PANDA:

Panda means "bamboo eater" in the language of the Himalayan people. I chirp, honk, and bark to express my mood. There are fewer of me in the world than any other kind of bear.

OCTOPUS:

Okay, okay, so I'm not a bear. I'm a cephalopod mollusk and live in the ocean!

KOALA BEAR:

I'm not really a bear, either! I'm a marsupial.

MORE BOOKS TO GET YOUR PAWS ON!

Cherrix, Amy. *Backyard Bears*. New York: Houghton Mifflin Harcourt, 2018.

Daly, Ruth, and Paula Smith. *Bringing Back the Grizzly Bear*. New York: Crabtree Publishing, 2018.

Eaton, Maxwell, III. *The Truth About Bears*. New York: Roaring Brook Press, 2018.

Emminizer, Theresa. *Grizzly Bears*. New York: PowerKids Press, 2020.

Froeb, Lori C. *I Am a Polar Bear*. San Diego: Silver Dolphin Books, 2019.

Grunbaum, Mara. *Black Bears*. New York: Children's Press, 2019.

Kenney, Karen Latchana. *Saving the Grizzly Bear*. Minneapolis: Pogo, 2019.

Laidlaw, Rob. *5 Bears*. Ontario: Fitzhenry & Whiteside, 2021.

Levy, Janey. *Hippo vs. Polar Bear*. New York: Gareth Stevens Publishing, 2018.

Petrillo, Lisa. *All About North American Black Bears*. Hallandale, Florida: Mitchell Lane Publishers, 2019.

Santos, Rita. *Polar Bears, Life at the Poles*. New York: Enslow Publishing, 2020.

Websites:

zoo.sandiegozoo.org/cams/panda-cam

nps.gov/subjects/bears/safety.htm

kids.nationalgeographic.com

bearbiology.org/bears-of-the-world/

Bears are big and powerful. We can be dangerous, especially if surprised or scared, or while caring for cubs. But we're helpful, too. Around the world, bears are losing habitat. Ice that Polar Bears need to live is melting. Fish that Brown Bears eat are disappearing. You can help us by telling others how important we are to the earth. Thanks, you are BEARY COOL!